insight text guide

Leon Furze

Born a Crime

Stories from a South African Childhood

Trevor Noah

First published in 2022.

Insight Publications Pty Ltd
3/350 Charman Road
Cheltenham VIC 3192
Australia
Tel: +61 3 8571 4950
Fax: +61 3 8571 0257
Email: books@insightpublications.com.au

www.insightpublications.com.au

A catalogue record for this book is available from the National Library of Australia

Trevor Noah's Born a Crime / Leon Furze

Leon Furze asserts the moral right to be identified as the author of this work.

ISBNs:
9781922771261 (print)
9781922771278 (digital)
9781922771285 (bundle: print + digital)

Cover design by Melisa Paredes

Printed in Australia by Ligare Book Printers

contents

CHARACTER MAP

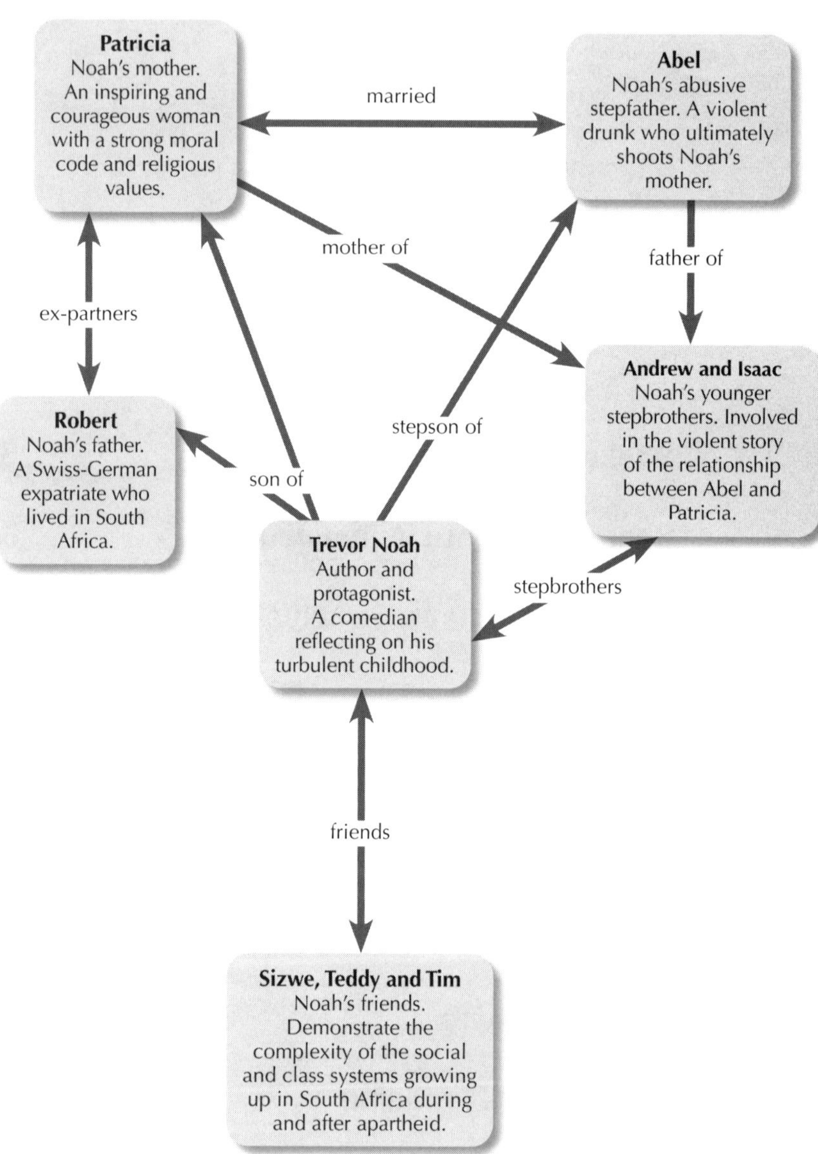

OVERVIEW

About the author

Trevor Noah was born in Johannesburg, South Africa in 1984, several years before the end of apartheid in the early 1990s. He is a television host, an author and a comedian who is most famous for his role as the host of the US late-night talk and satirical news television program *The Daily Show*.

Noah's early childhood is explored in great detail in *Born a Crime*, from the rationale behind the title of the book – the literal crime of race-mixing leading to his birth – through his school days and into young adulthood. The memoir focuses mainly on Noah's life *before* he became a successful comedian, though he does allude to his career – for example, when he visits his father, Robert, in his twenties. Noah's mother, a Xhosa woman named Patricia, raised him with her own mother in the township of Soweto, just outside Johannesburg. For much of his early childhood, Noah was kept hidden from the authorities because of his light skin colour.

Noah's career in news and entertainment began in South Africa in the early 2000s, with small roles in soap operas and on public television and radio (Encyclopedia Britannica, 'Trevor Noah', 2022). He performed stand-up routines for several years, gaining global recognition as a comedian, before relocating to the United States in 2011. Over the next few years, he appeared on several US talk shows, including *The Tonight Show* and the *Late Show with David Letterman*. Then, in 2015, Noah replaced Jon Stewart as the host of *The Daily Show*, a position that allowed him to combine his comedic chops with his love and skill for political commentary.

Born a Crime: Stories from a South African Childhood was first published in 2016, with an adapted version released for young readers. The book became a *New York Times* bestseller.

Synopsis

Trevor Noah's *Born a Crime* explores his memories of childhood and adolescence, both during and after apartheid. The book begins with anecdotes about Noah's childhood, focused particularly on his mother's religious nature and the impact of this on him as a boy. Throughout the text the chapters follow a similar format, featuring both general memories of life in South Africa and specific (and usually hilarious) anecdotes.

Noah progresses from his birth – evidence of a crime during apartheid when racial mixing was illegal – to his early preschool years and then into primary school. He explores how his skin colour presented barriers to him growing up, even when he was unaware of the racial divisions that existed in South Africa during and after apartheid. As he reaches primary school age, Noah begins to notice differences in colour, language and ethnicity.

Part I begins with stories about Noah's mother and ends with memories about his father Robert. It also introduces early memories of Noah's relationships with girls, education and the law – all of which were fraught with difficulties.

Part II continues through Noah's younger years, following him from primary school into high school and from one town to another. Many of the themes from Part I remain, including Noah's troubles with relationships, the bullying he experienced because of his skin colour, and the ways in which he used his language skills and obvious talents for getting into trouble. Part II includes the three-part series titled 'A young man's long, awkward, occasionally tragic, and frequently humiliating education in affairs of the heart', which explores in detail Noah's frequent mishaps in dating and romance.

Part III focuses on the years towards the end of Noah's schooling and into young adulthood. These were years when Noah spent much of his time with friends hanging out in the 'hood' of Alexandra, getting into trouble with the law for selling illegal copied CDs, fencing stolen items and hosting illegal street parties. This is also the part of the text in which the violence and crime Noah witnessed all his life becomes even more apparent. The story of his mother's relationship with Abel is also explored in much more detail, including Abel's terrifying violence. The text ends with the story of his mother's shooting by Abel, who faced minimal legal repercussions due to corrupt and ineffective laws and societal biases against women.

Character summaries

Trevor Noah

Trevor Noah is both the author and the protagonist, and should be viewed as a 'character' in his own text. Noah is witty, humorous and constantly getting himself into trouble. He is also shown to be kind-hearted and capable of great compassion, and he has an especially strong relationship with his mother. Noah's journey from childhood through adolescence to young adulthood is fraught with violence, crime and danger, but he manages to get through it with his sense of humour intact.

Patricia Nombuyiselo Noah

Patricia is Noah's mother, and the subject of much of the story. Patricia was born into poverty and worked incredibly hard to escape the life of her childhood. When she later decided to have a child of her own, it was in typically rebellious fashion. She had Noah with a white Swiss-German man, Robert, in spite of laws during apartheid preventing racial mixing. Patricia is characterised as stubborn, righteous, religious and fiercely protective of her children.

Robert

Robert is Noah's mysterious and secretive father, a white Swiss-German expatriate who lived in South Africa during apartheid. Noah did not get to spend much of his childhood with his father as the laws of apartheid forced them apart. Even so, Robert is shown to be a caring and attentive father where possible, and in later years follows Noah's career with great interest and obvious love.

Abel

Abel is introduced later in the text, first as Patricia's 'friend', and later as her husband and Noah's stepfather. Patricia also has two more children with Abel. Abel is charming but is also quickly revealed to be abusive and violent, particularly when drunk. The violence towards Patricia, in particular, escalates throughout the text, reaching a climax towards the end when he shoots her in the leg and head and then threatens to shoot the children and himself.

BACKGROUND & CONTEXT

Languages and ethnicities of South Africa

Language is an incredibly important part of Noah's writing, and his life. Throughout the text he describes how his aptitude for languages allowed him to be a chameleon, moving between different groups of people and sometimes getting him out of trouble. In South Africa, the Constitution recognises eleven official languages: Afrikaans, English, isiNdebele/ Ndebele, isiXhosa/Xhosa, isiZulu/Zulu, Sepedi / Sesotho sa Leboa, Sesotho/Sotho, Setswana/Tswana, siSwati/Swazi, Tshivenda/Venda and Xitsonga/Tsonga (Alexander 2021). Noah's primary languages are Xhosa and English, but he speaks many more, including German, Tsonga and Afrikaans.

Part of the reason for the eleven languages of South Africa is the diverse ethnic make-up of the country. Many of the classifications of ethnic groups in South Africa stem from the divisions put in place during apartheid. These include the broad definitions of black, white, coloured (mixed-race) and Indian. During the colonial era that preceded apartheid, and throughout apartheid itself, black South Africans were categorised into major ethnic groups such as Xhosa, Zulu and Sotho. The Zulu are the largest ethnic group in South Africa, followed by the Xhosa (the ethnic group of Noah's mother and her family). Of the white population, the majority are Afrikaans and the remainder primarily of Dutch or British origin.

Apartheid

Apartheid is an Afrikaans word that translates as 'apartness'. It is the name of the policy that governed the interactions between whites and non-whites in South Africa, lasting from 1948 to 1994. There were many policies and laws put in place by the minority white authorities, almost all of which were designed to strip black and other non-white South Africans of their rights. These laws controlled everything from work to relationships. *Born a Crime* includes an extract from the 1927 Immorality Act, which stipulated that it was a crime for white and black persons to have sex. These laws were expanded upon throughout apartheid, including the 1949 Prohibition of Mixed Marriages Act and the 1950 Immorality Amendment Act, which expanded the laws to apply to all non-white persons.

Under various land acts, land and property were stripped from black people and they were forced to live in specially designated areas, such as Soweto, where Noah spent his childhood. At best, these were poor and crowded urban areas. At worst, they were slums, such as those described by Noah in the latter parts of the book, where thousands upon thousands of people lived in poverty.

During apartheid, black citizens were denied the right to vote, access to education and healthcare services, and the protection of the law.

Nelson Mandela and the end of apartheid

Nelson Mandela was born in South Africa in 1918. He was the son of a local chief, but chose to renounce his claim to chieftaincy in order to become a lawyer. In 1944 he joined the African National Congress (ANC), becoming leader of its Youth League (Encyclopedia Britannica, 'Nelson Mandela', 2022). He opposed the laws of apartheid and the ruling National Party, against which he engaged in acts of sabotage and guerrilla warfare. In 1964 Mandela was sentenced to life imprisonment. He served eighteen years at the prison on Robben Island, six years at the maximum-security Pollsmoor Prison, in an attempt to curtail his influence on younger activists, and two years at Victor Verster Prison. In 1990, partially as a result of international political pressure, Mandela was released. He became head of the ANC and began talks with President Frederik Willem de Klerk to end apartheid.

In 1994 Nelson Mandela was elected president of South Africa. Following his election, he instituted many laws and policies to redress the harms done during apartheid, including an investigation into the human rights abuses that had occurred. After his period as president ended in 1999, Mandela continued to play an active role in politics and human rights advocacy in South Africa and internationally. Mandela died in 2013, aged ninety-five.

South Africa after apartheid

Trevor Noah was ten years old when apartheid ended, but it had been in place since long before he was born. Although Nelson Mandela heralded a great victory for black South Africans, the 'Bloodless Revolution' that is remembered worldwide appeared very different to the young Noah. The violence that had been institutionalised through laws and policies, separating not just non-whites from whites but different ethnicities within the black community, continued long after apartheid officially ended.

There are long-lasting economic and political ramifications from the protracted period of apartheid. More than half of the population of South Africa lives in poverty, and the vast majority of those people are black, coloured and non-white (Malik 2021). The education systems put in place during apartheid to oppress black citizens have resulted in nationally low levels of literacy and employment, and Noah himself reflects later in the text about the 'black tax' that follows black people through generations.

Although the laws of apartheid were repealed, there remain issues with a violent and controversial police force. Reports of police brutality are frequent, and South African police forces are alleged to kill twice as many people per year as police in the US. Noah reflects throughout the text on his own run-ins with the law, and there is a very real sense of threat when his mother warns him that they would kill him.

Although Noah's text is often light-hearted and humorous, the lasting effects of apartheid are clear throughout. Noah's own poverty and frequent misdemeanours and crimes are a reflection of the society in which he grew up and the long-term impact of the policies that were designed to oppress non-white people in South Africa.

GENRE, STRUCTURE & LANGUAGE

Genre

It would be appropriate to refer to *Born a Crime* as either an autobiography or a memoir. Both genres feature stories told by the author about their own life and recounts of events that happened to and around the author. However, autobiographies are typically more formal, and move in chronological order from birth up to the present. As Noah's text focuses on a specific part of his life – childhood and adolescence – and as it is made up of anecdotes and memories that sometimes jump around chronologically, the term 'memoir' may be more suitable.

Memoirs also have an element of creativity that the term 'autobiography' lacks. A reader would expect an autobiography to be very factual and well-researched, just like a biography written about another person. Memoirs, on the other hand, may dwell on certain stories, giving them greater importance in the overall narrative. Because memories are fallible, it is also more likely that stories have been exaggerated. In the case of *Born a Crime*, this is even more likely, as it is a humorous text; it is probable that some of Noah's stories have been embellished for comic effect. This does not mean that they are fictional, however. In a memoir, all the events are based in truth; however, some may be conflations of more than one real event, or characters may be comprised of several individuals. Without an author's commentary – or a very detailed critical analysis – it is impossible to tell.

Memoirs are also often thematic, as is the case with *Born a Crime*, which focuses on several prominent themes such as poverty, racism, relationships and crime. These themes are the anchor point for an engaging narrative. Unlike autobiographies, which are usually told chronologically, memoirs might introduce moments from elsewhere in time through flashbacks, flashforwards, or small vignettes or anecdotes. This happens frequently in *Born a Crime*; for example, in the first part of the text there is a sudden move from Noah's childhood to a moment from his early twenties when he reunites with his father. This abrupt jump in time does not distract the reader from the childhood stories because it fits with the theme of father–son relationships being explored at that moment in the text.

Finally, memoirs are always told in the first person, and are often more emotional than autobiographies. This works well for *Born a Crime* because it allows Noah to explore both the positive and negative emotions he experienced growing up in South Africa. From fear, guilt and shame, through to happiness, love and joy, Noah is able to take readers on a journey through the story of his life.

Structure

Born a Crime is divided into three parts that loosely conform to the three stages of Noah's life from early childhood through to adolescence. Beginning in Part I with his birth, the text moves through preschool, primary school and high school, and into adolescence. Where Part I deals mostly with the circumstances around Noah's birth – including chapters with detailed information about his parents, Patricia and Robert – Part II pays more attention to his relationships. The 'A young man's … education in affairs of the heart' chapters in Part II function as separate vignettes – short, evocative accounts of his relationships, with all their mishaps and failures. Part III deals mostly with Noah's older adolescent years into young adulthood, going through his time spent in the 'hood' of Alex, his criminal activities and arrests, and ultimately his mother's shooting.

Within each chapter there is often a similar structure, with the chapter divided between broader commentaries on social, racial and political aspects of life in South Africa and short personal anecdotes. Most chapters feature a main story or anecdote, which forms the basis for the title of that chapter; for example, 'Run' is centred on a story of Noah having to run from the Xhosa bus drivers who threatened his mother and her children; 'Chameleon' refers to Noah's ability to blend in through language; and 'Fufi' is focused on a story of Noah's first love: his dog Fufi.

As mentioned above, the structure of the memoir is not entirely chronological. 'Run' is set when Noah is nine years old. It is followed by 'Born a crime', which focuses on his birth and his parents' lives before he was born. The third chapter, 'Trevor, pray', moves to Noah as a five-year-old. Although the memories jump around, it is easy to follow the overall narrative of Noah's life due to his natural ability as a storyteller.

Before (or after) each chapter, there is also a short passage that acts as a lead-in, provides context or sometimes offers a different perspective; for example, immediately before 'Run' is a passage on apartheid and the tension between the Xhosa and Zulu, which helps to explain the anecdote of getting thrown from the bus. Before 'The mulberry tree', in which Noah is bullied badly because of his skin colour, there is a passage explaining the position of coloured people in South African society. Sometimes, these short passages provide a more personal context; for example, before 'My mother's life' there is a brief passage explaining more about Patricia's religious views, which helps to provide some context for her reasons for staying married to the abusive Abel.

Language

The language in *Born a Crime* is informal, witty, sometimes coarse and often hilarious. Noah writes like a comedian, delivering punchlines and comic moments through his choice of words, his sentence structures and the overall construction of his writing. For example, in the opening chapter, Noah begins with a brief and evocative description of someone in a Hollywood movie getting thrown from a moving car. He then switches to internal thoughts in italics – '*That's rubbish*' – and punctuates the story with 'I was nine years old when my mother threw me out of a moving car' (p.5).

Throughout the text, Noah uses language that would be familiar to an adolescent boy growing up in South Africa. In fact, the amount of coarse language and descriptions of violence in the text led to the republication of the book in a 'younger readers' format; for example, words relating to 'shit' in 'Trevor, pray' were changed to 'poop'. Even so, the comedic elements of his memoir remain intact.

It is also important to note that *language* is a significant theme in the text. Noah is a gifted linguist and speaks multiple languages, including Xhosa, English and Afrikaans. He comments frequently on the importance of language in blending in, getting out of trouble, making friends and defusing conflict. It is safe to assume, therefore, that Noah's own language in this text is carefully crafted, with the words chosen for their particular effects.

CHAPTER-BY-CHAPTER ANALYSIS

Note: Each chapter in *Born a Crime* is bookended with a short contextual passage, often discussing the lasting impact of apartheid in South Africa. In these chapter summaries, the passage that *precedes* each chapter will be included in the summary.

Dedication and Immorality Act (pp.vi–vii)

Summary: *Acting as a short prologue or epigraph, the book begins with an extract from the 1927 Immorality Act.*

Born a Crime begins with a dedication from Trevor Noah to his mother (p.vi), who, aside from Noah himself, is the most important person in the text. To contextualise the 'crime' of his birth, Noah also includes an excerpt from the 1927 Immorality Act, which includes two points: forbidding European males from having 'illicit carnal intercourse' with 'a native female' and vice versa.

PART I

Chapter 1: Run (pp.5–17)

Summary: *Noah provides an anecdote about a dangerous bus ride and discusses the importance of religion; different religions and races; and post-apartheid violence.*

Part I begins with a contextual discussion of apartheid, in which Noah describes the 'genius of apartheid' (p.3) as convincing the black South Africans to turn on one another. Throughout the book, Noah explores the tensions that exist between various groups, particularly the Xhosa and the Zulu.

Like much of *Born a Crime*, 'Run' begins with a humorous anecdote. Noah's humour both underpins his later career as a comedian and belies the trauma of his childhood, offering a stark contrast to the violent reality in which he grew up. 'Run' also introduces a key idea in the text: the importance of religion. Noah explains that many black South Africans decided to 'give this Jesus thing a shot' (p.6) because they felt they needed saving from the colonisers. He goes on to explain how his childhood was filled with religion, with church visits at least four nights a week. The different churches – black, white and coloured – offered different perspectives on religion but also served as an alternative form of entertainment for the young Noah, who otherwise had 'very little exposure to popular culture' (p.7).

Throughout the book Noah weaves personal anecdotes and memories with a broader commentary on the social and racial tensions in South Africa. Noah reflects on how the 'Bloodless Revolution' (p.12) after apartheid was only bloodless for white people – following Nelson Mandela's release from prison, there was a lot of violence between the Zulu and Xhosa. In remembering his church visits, Noah focuses on one particular trip that resulted in his mother throwing him from a moving vehicle before jumping out herself while holding Noah's baby brother in order to escape the angry Zulu drivers. The chapter ends with Noah and his mother laughing through the pain.

Key point

Noah's humour does not minimise the very real violence and struggles of his childhood; it is used to highlight both the adversity he faced and the strength of his will to overcome those struggles. Throughout the text, dark and often disturbing memories are filtered through this lens of comedy.

Key vocabulary

Xhosa: the second-largest indigenous ethnic group in South Africa, with the second-most populous language, also called Xhosa.

Zulu: the largest ethnic group indigenous to South Africa, and known for their military expertise.

Q What is interesting or unusual about the structure of the book, based on the opening parts and this first chapter?

Chapter 2: Born a crime (pp.21–31)

Summary: *Noah reflects on being 'born a crime'; he discusses his mother and father's relationship; Noah's backstory illuminates aspects of apartheid.*

The chapter is preceded by more contextualising of apartheid, including its early origins in 1652 with the arrival of the Dutch East India Company at the Cape of Good Hope. Noah refers to apartheid as 'perfect racism' (p.19) and describes the way in which apartheid was distilled from several other forms of racist policy, including British Empire slavery, the American removal of native peoples to reservations, and segregation.

Recalling the Immorality Act that opens the text, this titular chapter reflects on the 'crime' of 'having sexual relations with a person of another race' (p.21). Noah comments that race-mixing 'doesn't merely challenge the system as unjust, it reveals the system as unsustainable and incoherent' (p.21).

Noah goes into the backstory of his mother and father's relationship. His mother was a 'rebel' (p.23) and spent time living in a secret flat in the neighbourhood of Hillbrow. Learning how to play the system from Xhosa prostitutes, Patricia eventually ended up in a relationship with a Swiss-German expatriate, Robert. Although she made it clear that she only wanted a child – and not the support of a father – Noah's father played a role in his childhood. Noah discusses how his pale skin colour made him noticeably different from other children, and how his family lived in constant fear he would be taken away by the government.

The chapter ends with Noah reflecting on how well he can cope with being alone, and his surprise when he finally learns that he and his mother 'could have left' South Africa (p.30).

Q Why do you think Noah's mother chooses to stay in South Africa, rather than leave like many other parents with coloured children?

Key vocabulary

Apartheid: the set of rules, laws and policies governing the separation of whites and non-whites in South Africa from 1948 to 1994.

Chapter 3: Trevor, pray (pp.35–47)

Summary: *Noah reflects on the power of prayer in his childhood, and tells a short story about one of his many childhood mishaps.*

Noah contextualises the blend of African ancestral religion and Christianity, including pointing out the persistent beliefs in witchcraft and shamanism. The chapter begins with an exploration both of religion and of the relationships between women and men in South Africa. An undercurrent of violence – common throughout the book – pervades the relationships between males and females from Noah's childhood. This includes both a misogynistic and patriarchal attitude from males like his uncle Dinky and retaliative violence from the women.

Because of his skin colour, Noah is treated as a particularly powerful source of prayer. The chapter ends with a hilarious anecdote about a five-year-old Noah defecating on a piece of newspaper in his house and the subsequent panic that his household has been cursed, reflecting the way in which traditional beliefs around witchcraft had merged with colonial Christianity.

Key point

The theme of religion and faith recurs throughout the book, particularly in reference to Noah's mother's spirituality.

Q What is the serious message underpinning Noah's very funny anecdote in this chapter?

Chapter 4: Chameleon (pp.51–9)

Summary: *Noah reflects on the power of language to break down barriers, or create them; he recalls his schooling and how a grasp of different languages enabled him to move between groups.*

Listening to the simulcast of American TV shows on the radio during his childhood, Noah realises that language both creates and breaks down barriers. He observes how a shared language can 'trick' racists, confusing them by breaking down racist preconceptions. Noah begins this chapter by remembering occasions in his youth when his grandmother refrained from beating him because she didn't know 'how to hit a white child' (p.52). Before he knew that his special treatment was because of his colour, he believed it was just because he was 'Trevor'. Noah soon learns, however, that despite his different appearance, he can become a chameleon by learning the different languages of those around him.

The main anecdote in this chapter centres on Noah's experiences at school, where he is placed, at first, into a classroom that has a majority of white students. At recess, in the yard, Noah sees that most of the school's students are black, and realises that the white students are actually in the minority overall.

After impressing his fellow students with his ability to speak back to them in their own languages, Noah decides to request to move into the B class, where the majority of the students are black. He comments at the end of the chapter that his experience at the school led him to identify as black: 'I'd never had to choose, but when I was forced to choose, I chose black' (p.59).

Q What is the link between language and race?

Q What do you think Noah means when he says, 'with the black kids, I just was' (p.59)?

Chapter 5: The second girl (pp.63–74)

Summary: *Noah reflects on the importance of education, as well as on his mother, his childhood and growing up in poverty.*

Preceding the chapter, Noah explores the way in which Bantu schools were constructed during apartheid in order to 'cripple the black mind' (p.61). Education is another recurrent theme throughout this text; in addition to Patricia's opinion on the importance of learning, which is offered at various times in Noah's life, education during apartheid is explored more holistically.

The chapter begins with more backstory of Noah's mother, including her stubborn, defiant nature. Noah's mother received some formal education through a mission school run by a white pastor, where she was taught English. She passed the language down to Noah, teaching him English as his first language.

Noah recalls how he and his mother moved to Eden Park, a coloured neighbourhood where Patricia hoped they would have a better life. Thinking of his childhood, Noah remembers both good and bad times. He states that 'food ... was always the measure of how good or bad things were going' (p.71). Despite his mother's frugality and their lack of money – they sometimes had to eat soup made of dog bones – Noah has fond memories of his mother taking him to places like the drive-through cinema and for trips through 'fancy white neighbourhoods' (p.73).

Most importantly for Noah were the lessons his mother taught him, namely that 'the ghetto is not the world' (p.74).

Q How does Noah explore both the good and bad times of his own childhood? Did the good outweigh the bad, or vice versa?

Key vocabulary

Bantu: a colonial word derived from the Zulu word for people; an offensive term used to describe black people as a group.

Key point

Once again Noah focuses a great deal of attention on his mother. Patricia was a stubborn and wilful child who grew into a protective and determined mother, and Noah affirms that he owes much of his success to the things he learned from her.

Chapter 6: Loopholes (pp.77–91)

Summary: *Noah recalls his early life as an unruly child; he shares an anecdote about his relationship with his mother; his love of fire gets him in big trouble.*

The chapter is preceded by a short contextual piece reflecting on the absurdity of apartheid, and the 'fatal flaws' that were there from the start (p.75). 'Loopholes' begins with another series of recollections about Noah's childhood, focusing this time on his unruly behaviour. Noah's many misdeeds included his hyperactive running away, 'general naughtiness and misbehaviour' (p.78), and his love of fire and knives.

As with other chapters, 'Loopholes' is peppered with short anecdotes, including the time Noah burnt off his eyebrows with a box of firecrackers and the time his mother denied that he was her child because he was being irritating in the grocery store. The comedic relationship between Noah and his mother continues to provide much of the humour in the book.

Noah and his mother become so antagonistic towards one another – due to Noah's constant misbehaviour – that they resort to writing each other letters to avoid having verbal arguments. Still keeping the tone lighthearted, the chapter takes a darker turn as Noah discusses the beatings his mother would give him for serious indiscretions, and the corporal punishment meted out by the Catholic school nuns.

Following a story about his expulsion from school, the chapter ends with Noah's biggest childhood misdeed: 'burning down a white person's house' (p.90). Despite the severity of the incident, Noah maintains his innocence, stating blithely that 'there were matches and there was a magnifying glass and there was a mattress and then, clearly, a series of unfortunate events' (p.90).

Q Do you think that Noah's claim of innocence is fair? Why or why not?

Chapter 7: Fufi (pp.95–100)

Summary: *Noah remembers his family pets.*

In this short chapter, Noah recalls how his mother brought home two black cats – a dangerous thing in a society in which animals were seen as a mark of witchcraft. Although she thought it would be okay, the cats are killed, skinned and hung from the front gate with the word *Heks* (witch in Afrikaans) written on the wall.

Replacing the cats, they eventually get two dogs: Panther and Fufi. Fufi is 'beautiful but stupid' (p.97) and the love of Noah's life. The dog is also his 'first heartbreak' (p.100), briefly leaving Noah for another boy before his mother purchases him back. The chapter ends with Noah's reflection on what Fufi taught him about love and betrayal.

Q What is the purpose of this short chapter?

Chapter 8: Robert (pp.103–11)

Summary: *Noah recalls facts from his father's life; the two are reunited after a long separation.*

Robert was a Swiss-German expatriate who lived in South Africa: that is almost the full extent of what Noah knew about his mysterious and 'extremely secretive' (p.111) father. Robert was also very anti-racist, going out of his way to open a restaurant that would serve both blacks and whites at a time when most establishments were segregated.

Noah saw his father weekly during his childhood, but when he turned thirteen his father moved to Cape Town, and his mother had married the alcoholic and abusive Abel, who made it difficult for Noah to see his father. Their contact slowly diminished until, by the time Noah was in his early twenties, he had stopped seeing his father altogether. When they finally reconnected, however, it was like picking up where they had left off, with his father 'treating [him] exactly the way he'd treated [him] as a thirteen-year-old boy' (p.109). Falling back on his skills as a TV presenter and host, Noah tries to interview his father to learn more about him; it doesn't work, so instead he decides to just spend time with him to learn more organically about his life.

Q Compare the relationship Noah has with his mother and with his father. Do you think his estrangement from his father bothered him? Why or why not?

Key vocabulary

Expatriate: someone who has moved to live outside their native country.

Key point

Noah has a complex relationship with each of his parents. While his mother raised him and shaped the way he sees the world, his father also provided some of the defining characteristics of Noah's personality and outlook on life, including a distaste for racism and an inability to understand why racist people would go to Africa in the first place.

PART II

Chapter 9: The mulberry tree (pp.117–26)

Summary: *Noah discusses being an outcast; a bullying incident at the mulberry tree escalates into dangerous territory.*

The short passage preceding this chapter introduces the 'curse' (p.115) of being coloured: a lack of clearly defined cultural heritage. During Noah's childhood, this curse was realised in his home town of Eden Park, where the coloured children discriminated against each other as much as the whites against the blacks.

Noah explores the absurdities of apartheid law, commenting on how coloured people could be 'promoted to white' (p.118) if their appearance was sufficiently white. The status of coloured people as '*amperbaas:* "the almost-boss"' (p.118) meant that they were stranded between the privilege of white people and the communities of black people.

Noah reflects on how he was 'bullied all the time' (p.121) and proceeds to tell the story at the mulberry tree, when a number of other children – also coloured – call him a 'bushman' and pelt him with ripe and unripe mulberries (p.122).

The incident escalates when Noah goes home and recounts it to his mother's boyfriend – later his stepfather – the drunk and abusive Abel. Noah recalls with horror how Abel took to the lead bully with a tree branch, beating the twelve-year-old boy and forcing him to apologise. The chapter reflects not only on the nature of being an outcast, but also on the violence of Noah's childhood.

Q What do you think was worse for Noah: the experience of the incident at the mulberry tree itself, or the aftermath with Abel? Explain your choice.

Chapter 10: A young man's long, awkward, occasionally tragic, and frequently humiliating education in the affairs of the heart, part I: Valentine's Day (pp.129–33)

Summary: *Noah learns about Valentine's Day; he is encouraged to ask out a girl; he has his heart broken for the first time.*

After a reflection about his mother's relationship advice and guidance on how to treat women, this chapter explores one of Noah's early experiences with relationships. At twelve years old Noah had never heard of Valentine's Day, but he is quickly encouraged by the other – white – students to ask a coloured girl to be his valentine. As much as relationships, this chapter is also about race.

Noah plucks up the courage to ask out Maylene and she says yes. Unfortunately, when Valentine's Day arrives Noah is 'devastated' (p.133) when Maylene informs him that she has been asked out by the popular white boy Leonardo.

This chapter begins a series of reminiscences in the text about Noah's ill-fated relationships.

Key point

Until now, the only relationships Noah has explored are with his mother and his dog Fufi. Part II in the text marks a new stage in Noah's life: adolescence, and with it an increased range of experiences with relationships.

Chapter 11: Outsider (pp.137–41)

Summary: *Noah recalls his first years of high school; he begins a lucrative career buying food for other students.*

In *Born a Crime*, being an outsider is closely linked to both race and poverty. Noah reflects on his first years at Sandringham High School, which have a different focus to his earlier recollections of primary school. While at primary school he noticed the differences between populations of white and black students, at high school he finds much more nuanced groups.

Because his school had a very mixed population, the distinction between racial groups was less clear. Noah felt the most affinity for the 'poor black kids' (pp.138–9). It was partly Noah's own poverty – unable to afford petrol, or sometimes even food – that led him to come up with an ingenious way to make money: he was fast, so at the end of assembly he would race to the canteen to place orders for himself and others. He learned both that 'time is money' and that he could use his status as an outsider to move between social groups as a 'chameleon' (p.140).

Key point

This is one of the moments in the memoir in which Noah indicates the importance of humour in his life. He understands that it is a bridge to joining other social groups.

Chapter 12: A young man's long, awkward, occasionally tragic, and frequently humiliating education in the affairs of the heart, part II: the crush (pp.145–9)

Summary: *Noah continues to navigate the world of teenage relationships.*

In the second of three chapters on relationships, Noah reflects on a missed opportunity with a girl he was friendly with during high school. The chapter is preceded by a short piece that articulates that the only regrets Noah has are for things he didn't do. This chapter picks up on that thread through an anecdote about his friendship with Zaheera, and the fact that she left for the US before he had a chance to ask her out.

Once again, Noah's stories of his childhood relationships are funny and revealing, and demonstrate his unfortunate luck with girls.

Chapter 13: Colorblind (pp.153–9)

Summary: *Noah describes his friendship with Teddy; the two of them get into trouble with the law.*

At Sandringham, Noah meets Teddy – another troublemaker like himself. The two become good friends, and get into trouble both inside and outside of school. Noah describes some of their escapades, ending with an anecdote about stealing alcohol-filled chocolates from a cinema.

On one occasion, Noah is caught with his arm through the bars of the cinema by a security guard. Noah and Teddy run away; the two are separated and Noah escapes through a hole in the fence of an alley.

Later, Noah discovers that Teddy has been caught, arrested for shoplifting and ultimately expelled from school. Teddy does not tell the authorities that Noah had been with him, and so he escapes any punishment.

In the principal's office, Noah watches in horror as Mr Friedman plays a video tape of security camera footage clearly showing both Teddy and Noah running from the guards. However, because Teddy is black and Noah much lighter-skinned, the low-quality camera equipment overcompensates, and Noah appears white.

The chapter ends with Noah's reflection that the people were so blinded by their 'construct of race that they could not see that the white person they were looking for was sitting right in front of them' (p.159).

Q What 'bigger picture' idea is Noah commenting on in this chapter, using the anecdote of Teddy's arrest?

Chapter 14: A young man's long, awkward, occasionally tragic, and frequently humiliating education in the affairs of the heart, part III: the dance (pp.163–79)

Summary: *Noah is introduced to a beautiful girl; he takes her to a dance, but only then realises the language barrier that stands between them.*

The chapter is preceded by another discussion of language in South Africa, with a reflection on the eleven official languages of the country. Noah then introduces Tim, another of his childhood friends and one of the 'two middlemen working for [him] in [his bootleg] CD business' (p.164). Tim was 'a real hustler' (p.164), and got Noah into a number of scrapes, including one that resulted in him having to pretend to be an American rapper at a performance for which Tim had been paid.

As part of a deal, Tim introduces Noah to Babiki, a beautiful, shy girl from downtown. Noah, Tim and Babiki meet on a number of occasions, and they even convince Abel to lend Noah his BMW to drive Babiki to the matriculation (matric) dance.

When the night of the dance arrives, Abel is drunk and refuses to lend the BMW. Noah arrives late to pick up an irritated Babiki, and they drive to the dance in silence. Once there, she refuses to get out of the car.

Ultimately, Noah works out that Babiki cannot speak English, only Pedi, which Noah cannot speak. He realises he has never had a conversation with Babiki without Tim acting as the middleman. Eventually he resigns himself to driving her home, and to make things even more confusing she kisses him before getting out of the car.

Key point

This is another of Noah's failed romantic encounters, and the third and final chapter in the 'long, awkward, occasionally tragic' series. These three chapters outline much of the teenage awkwardness Noah experienced growing up. Although the language barrier is a specific problem, many readers will be able to identify with Noah's moments of rejection and awkwardness.

PART III

Chapter 15: Go Hitler! (pp.185–99)

Summary: *Noah receives a CD burner, which changes his life; he grows a business, first producing CDs, then DJing at parties; a member of his dance crew inadvertently causes a great deal of offence.*

Noah receives a CD burner from Daniel after working for him and Bolo selling bootleg CDs. The burner enables him to make his own CDs, which in turn allows him to make more money than he has had access to in the past. His huge library of downloaded music also leads to an unexpected career as a party DJ.

As his success at parties grows, Noah and his friend Sizwe decide they need a dance crew to perform for them. They enlist the help of a boy named Hitler. Noah reflects on the naming of some children in South Africa, pointing out that their parents have not received a Western education and that, despite the horrors of the Holocaust, the name Hitler is essentially meaningless.

After a series of successful events, Noah and his dance crew are invited to play at a diversity day at a Jewish school. As soon as Hitler begins to dance and the crew chants his name, the incensed teachers literally pull the plug and kick them out of the school.

Key point

Noah's reflections in this chapter are likely to be uncomfortable for a Western reader who has been educated about the horrors of the Holocaust. Nonetheless, his observations are accurate: to the Africans who have not learned about the atrocities of World War II, the name Hitler carries no negative associations. Furthermore, Noah highlights the fact that atrocities have been committed in Africa that Westerners would have no understanding of themselves.

Q Read page 195. What is the tone of Noah's arguments here? Is he being humorous, as elsewhere in the book, or is this passage noticeably different? Why?

Chapter 16: The cheese boys (pp.203–24)

Summary: *Noah and Sizwe hang out in the hood; Noah discusses poverty, wealth and crime.*

This chapter is centred on the township of Alexandra, called Alex, where to this day over 200 000 people live in shacks built one on top of another. Noah's friend Sizwe, who lives in Alex, invites him to 'the hood' (p.204). Noah describes the township in vivid detail on page 205, including the sights, sounds and smells. He comments on the similarities between the hood and popular American hip-hop culture, and of the constant and sometimes deadly violence.

Noah introduces the idea of the 'cheese boys' (p.207), a slang term used for anyone with money because cheese was the most expensive item on a burger. These 'cheese boys' are also classed based on where they live – for example, Sizwe and his crew live in East Bank, and are therefore considered wealthier than others in Alex.

Noah moves on from the distinctions of poverty and wealth to talk about the ever-present crime in Alexandra, including their own small contributions selling pirated CDs on the street corner. He describes Sizwe's ability to 'flip' money, taking sixty rand and turning it into 200, and also how mothers in the hood would buy items from Noah and Sizwe because they looked more respectable than 'some crackhead' (p.215).

Reflecting on the nature of hustling, Noah understands that although it felt like they were constantly moving, they were never really going anywhere. The chapter ends with a memory of being thrown in jail overnight, and Noah's acknowledgement that he was fundamentally different from others in Alex because he had the choice to leave.

Key point

Crime and punishment are further key ideas in this text and are closely related to Noah's commentaries on both race and poverty.

Q Why do you think Noah chooses to spend time in the hood, even though he can leave any time he wants?

Chapter 17: The world doesn't love you (pp.227–43)

Summary: *Noah goes to jail for the second time; he tries to hide it from his mother.*

In this penultimate chapter Noah once again recalls being taken to jail – this time for a full week. He takes a car from Abel's garage yard, puts a set of numberplates onto it and drives away. When he is pulled over and the police officer checks the numberplates in the system, Noah realises that he has made a big mistake. However, he is more concerned about his mother finding out than about going to jail.

Noah explores the difference between jail and prison and thinks about how he has to act tough in order to make the other prisoners afraid of him, deflecting his own fear. Taken to a holding cell before his hearing, he is once again forced to choose between the coloured group, the blacks and the whites. He chooses this time to go to the white men because they are the least threatening.

When he is finally freed he realises that his mother knew all along and was in fact the one who paid his bail. The chapter ends with his mother telling him, 'When I beat you, I'm trying to save you. When they beat you, they're trying to kill you' (p.243).

Q There are many stories in this collection about Noah's mother beating and punishing him – do you think he bears any negative feelings towards her because of that?

Chapter 18: My mother's life (pp.247–82)

Summary: *Noah reflects on his mother and Abel; Noah's childhood stories come to an end with a violent twist.*

Violence is never far from the surface throughout Noah's memoir, and this final chapter is no different. Noah returns to stories of the most influential person in his life: his mother, Patricia. The chapter begins with an explanation of how Patricia met and eventually married Abel, the alcoholic, abusive mechanic who became Noah's stepfather and was the father of his two stepbrothers.

Noah goes into detail about the patriarchal Tsonga culture in which Abel grew up, pointing out how Patricia did not fit the stereotypical role of docile, subservient woman and wife. This was a source of embarrassment and shame to Abel, and he did not react well to Patricia's behaviour. Eventually, Abel's abuse escalated to hitting Patricia, and later Noah. In between stories of how great a mechanic Abel was, Noah reveals the dark truth about the man who was 'a saint in the streets' (p.271) but a monster behind closed doors.

Aged forty-four, his mother had a second child with Abel: Isaac. Eventually, Patricia left Abel and Noah moved away to focus on his comedy career. Then Andrew – Patricia and Abel's first son – called Noah and told him that their mother had been shot.

The story of Patricia's shooting is told at a breathless pace, and Noah remembers how he cried more than he had ever cried in his life. By some miracle the bullet that entered the back of her head comes out of her left nostril, having missed her spinal cord and major arteries along the way. Patricia survives, and Noah ends the book with a final reflection in the style of an epilogue about his mother's continued and fervent belief in Jesus (pp.283–5).

Key vocabulary

Patriarchy: a societal system in which males hold power and females are largely excluded from it.

Key point

In retrospect, it seems as though Abel's tendency towards anger and violence was always leading to this point. However, the stories of domestic violence and abuse in this book do not follow a straightforward, linear pattern: the relationships between the people in Noah's life are complex, and he often reflects on the fact that he was too young and too inexperienced to really know what was going on at the time. One of the important features of memoirs and autobiographies is that they allow authors to both remember and to reflect, adding a layer of wisdom and experience to their childhood memories.

CHARACTERS & RELATIONSHIPS

Trevor Noah

Key quotes

'The doctors took her up to the delivery room, cut open her belly, and reached in and pulled out a half-white, half-black child who violated any number of laws, statutes, and regulations – I was born a crime.' (p.26)

'I was the anomaly wherever we lived.' (p.117)

'I grew up in a world of violence, but I myself was never violent at all. Yes, I played pranks and set fires and broke windows, but I never attacked people. I never hit anyone. I was never angry.' (p.262)

Although this is a nonfiction text, it is still useful to view the people involved as 'characters' constructed by the author. In this respect, Noah is the protagonist of the text, the main character through whose eyes we see all the action and conflict. The reader relies on Noah to tell the truth of his memories growing up in South Africa, and memories are often fallible or exaggerated. Still, we have no other perspective and so we take Noah's words at face value and assume that all the hilarious and often dangerous events of his life unfolded as written.

Noah was literally 'born a crime' because he was 'a half-white, half-black child who violated any number of laws, statutes, and regulations' (p.26). The strict laws against race-mixing under apartheid meant that his mother, Patricia, and father, Robert, could have been arrested if the authorities had found out about the birth. This presents a profound challenge for Noah throughout his childhood as he is simultaneously aware of his different skin colour, but unable to understand why such divisions exist. He was not able to spend much time with his father, and his mother admitted that she wanted a baby more for her own sake than to raise a family. Noah spent much of his childhood alone, to the extent that even to this day he has to 'remember to be with people' (p.30).

This part of his nature – his life as an outcast – stays with him for much of his childhood. Later in the text he states, 'I was the anomaly wherever we lived' (p.117). Looking back on his childhood as an adult, Noah understands that a large part of his isolation was due to the systemic design of apartheid. Apartheid was built in order to segregate those of different races and to turn black South Africans against one another. Absurd rules meant that individuals could be classed as white based on their appearance rather than their genetic heritage, and 'other colored people hated [Trevor] because of [his] whiteness' (p.121). At the same time, Noah sometimes found it hard to mix with black children, and never felt like he fit in with white children either.

Aside from his colour, one of Noah's primary concerns in the text is growing up in poverty, and how this shaped him as a young person. Noah describes himself as a natural capitalist and frequently justifies his criminal activities – including selling bootleg CDs and obviously stolen goods – as 'hustle'. Throughout the text it certainly seems that, from Noah's perspective at least, his crimes are justified, given the systemic and societal issues that led to so many South Africans living in poverty.

Noah is also exposed to a lot of violence growing up, from the domestic abuse he witnesses between family members, to violence on the streets, and ultimately the shooting of his own mother by his stepfather, Abel. Despite all this, Noah remains non-violent himself, saying, 'I never attacked people. I never hit anyone. I was never angry' (p.262). This is because he 'saw the futility of violence, the cycle that just repeats itself, the damage that's inflicted on people that they in turn inflict on others' (p.262). Noah's experiences of violence as a young adult may have hardened some of his attitudes towards life, but the values instilled in him by his mother, his sense of humour and his overall temperament meant that he never grew into a violent person like those around him.

Key point

Noah demonstrates that although we are shaped by the events in our childhood, they do not have to define us: we have a choice over how we act out our own lives. This is clear in his response to violence, in his escape from poverty, and in the ways in which he breaks free of the limiting education system and lack of opportunities for coloured children in South Africa.

Patricia Nombuyiselo Noah

Key quotes

'There were times when she literally ate dirt. She would go down to the river, take the clay from the riverbank, and mix it with the water to make a grayish kind of milk. She'd drink that to feel full.' (p.65)

'My mom did what school didn't. She taught me how to think.' (p.68)

'Beautiful on the outside, beautiful on the inside.' (p.248)

Aside from Noah himself, his mother, Patricia, is the most important character in this text. Her impact on Noah's life is apparent from the very start of the book, and he spends time delving into her history, her childhood, and her relationships with both his father, Robert, and stepfather, Abel. It is also clear that Patricia plays an important role in aspects of Noah's life such as education, religion and even romance.

Patricia Noah was always a 'rebel' (p.23), rejecting the expectations placed upon her both as a woman and as a black person in South Africa. Her rebellious nature is evident from early on in the text, where Noah describes his mother's relationship with the Swiss-German expatriate Robert, despite the laws preventing unions between blacks and whites. Patricia decided to have a child with Robert despite the laws, and so Noah is 'born a crime'. Patricia explains to Noah that she 'chose' to have him because she wanted 'something that would love [her] unconditionally in return' (p.63), and though sometimes it seems as though Noah may disappoint or frustrate her, her love for him is clear.

It also seems as though Patricia had a child in order to give them the kind of life she could not have. From growing up in poverty – 'there were times when she literally ate dirt' (p.65) – Patricia goes out of her way to ensure that Noah has both an education and life experiences. Noah points out that his mother's name – Patricia Nombuyiselo Noah – means 'She Who Gives Back' (p.67) and he returns to this aspect of her personality throughout the text. He notes that, despite his misbehaviour, her attitude is always, 'I chose you, kid. I brought you into this world, and I'm going to give you everything I never had' and that she saw it as her job to feed Noah's 'body … spirit … [and] mind' (p.71). Patricia was also very conscious of the racial inequalities in South Africa and 'raised [Trevor] like a white kid – not white culturally, but in the sense of believing that the world was [his] oyster' (p.73). By teaching him English as a first language and sending him to the best schools she could, allowing him to mix with white students, Patricia aimed to give Noah the opportunities she never had.

Patricia also provides Noah with advice about relationships and women, whether he wants it or not. She teaches him that 'being a man is not what you have, it's who you are. Being more of a man doesn't mean your woman has to be less than you' (p.127). Although she fails to follow her own advice – marrying the abusive Abel and staying with him despite his multiple drunken assaults – Patricia teaches Noah that he does not have to act like the archetypal masculine figure that the patriarchal African society would suggest. Although sometimes her lessons are strict, with 'tough love, lectures, punishment, and hidings' (p.227), the reader never gets the impression that Noah resents any of his mother's input into his life.

In *Born a Crime*, Noah gets into trouble with the law on multiple occasions. Once again it is his mother's advice and teaching that he comes back to. She tells him that 'one day you're going to get arrested, and when you do, don't call me. I'll tell the police to lock you up just to teach you a lesson' (p.228). Despite this, she also makes sure that Noah knows the police don't 'love' him, and that 'when they beat you, they're trying to kill you' (p.243). Ultimately, Noah realises that, unlike some of his friends in the 'hood' of Alexandra, he has a choice to leave – a choice that his mother has provided him.

Noah ends his book with a series of reflections on his mother's shooting, and some final words on Patricia's impact on his life. He affirms that, 'as headstrong and independent as my mom is, she remains the woman who gives back' (p.258).

Key point

Patricia and Noah's relationship is complex. Her strict punishment of his behaviour would be largely unacceptable in modern-day Western society, but in this text Noah uses his trademark sense of humour to make light of it, comparing his relationship with his mother to that between cartoon characters Tom and Jerry. It is difficult at times to read about the violence in Noah's life, despite it being clear that he loves and respects his mother very much.

Robert

Key quotes

'Too many men grow up without their fathers, so they spend their lives with a false impression of who their father is and what a father should be.' (p.101)

'He's very Swiss, clean and particular and precise.' (p.104)

'He was caring and devoted, attentive to detail, always a card on my birthday, always my favorite food and toys when I came for a visit. But at the same time he was a closed book.' (p.107)

Noah's Swiss-German father, Robert, is secretive and 'a complete mystery' (p.103). At the start of Chapter 8, the main chapter focused on his father's life, Noah details what he learned about his father from his mother. This includes the fact that he was never married, and that when he moved to Johannesburg he exploited a legal loophole to open one of the first integrated restaurants, serving both blacks and whites. Because of the laws pertaining to race-mixing, Noah grew up pretending that he did not have a father. Noah was only permitted to visit on Sunday afternoons, and as he grew older even those meetings faded away.

Patricia and Robert's relationship was as much a product of her rebellious nature as it was of romance, and her decision to have a child with him was not made because Patricia wanted to start a family with Robert specifically. Nonetheless, despite the unusual circumstances and the laws preventing their interactions, Noah describes Robert as 'caring and devoted' and 'attentive to detail' (p.107), always remembering birthdays and favourite foods.

When Noah and his father drift apart – partially due to his mother's relationship with Abel – Noah does not seem to feel a great deal of regret. However, his mother encourages him to search for his father and get to know him again. Ten years after their separation, and after Noah has begun his career as a comedian, he seeks out and eventually tracks down his father. He writes, 'It felt like this ten-year gap in my life closed right up in an instant, like only a day had passed since I'd last seen him' (p.109). Noah and his father pick up where they had left off, right down to his father producing Noah's favourite childhood foods. In a moving scene, his father shows Noah newspaper clippings he has kept of Noah's shows and public appearances, and the two reconnect. Still, the chapter ends with Noah repeating to his father that 'all I know is that you're extremely secretive' (p.111).

Abel

Key quotes

'I didn't know him that well, but one thing I did know about him was that he had a temper. Very charming when he wanted to be, incredibly funny, but fuck he could be mean.' (p.123)

'I didn't know the word "sinister" then, but if I had I probably would have used it. "There's just something not right about him. I don't trust him. I don't think he's a good person."' (p.249)

'I always thought of Abel as a cobra: calm, perfectly still, then explosive.' (p.254)

Abel does not appear in the text properly until we are well into Noah's stories of his late childhood and early adolescence. After his mother's relationship with Robert, Abel is the next serious man in her life. Initially, the young Noah sees Abel as just his mother's 'cool friend' (p.249), but it quickly becomes apparent to both Noah and the reader that there is something 'sinister' about him, and that he is clearly not a 'good person' (p.249).

Abel's later violence is foreshadowed in some of the earliest scenes that mention him. Noah writes that 'he had a temper' (p.123) and in a seemingly off-handed comment remarks that 'Abel didn't have a gun yet; he bought that later' (p.126). Abel's gun proves to be a crucial element of Noah's book, but it does not reappear until the very end of the memoir, when Abel's violence escalates to the point of shooting Patricia and threatening to also shoot the children and himself. It is Abel's tendency to resort quickly to violence that makes him such an unsettling character. Noah writes, 'I always thought of Abel as a cobra: calm, perfectly still, then explosive' (p.254). Abel's violence towards a child in 'The mulberry tree' (pp.117–26) proves Noah's impressions correct. Abel is also characterised by his drinking, and his conformity to the patriarchal norms of African society, in which a man has complete control over his wife.

Ultimately Abel and Patricia's relationship is doomed, even after they have a son of their own, Andrew. Patricia stays with Abel for, in Noah's opinion at least, much longer than she should, and it ends in violence and near tragedy.

Key point

The violence that Abel demonstrates towards his wife and others in this text is emblematic of the violence Noah witnessed growing up. Throughout the text Noah reflects on this violence with detachment, often suggesting that it is a by-product of societal and political problems rather than a fault with the individuals themselves.

Teddy, Tim and Sizwe

Key quotes

'At Sandringham I got to know this one kid, Teddy. Funny guy, charming as hell.' (p.153)

'Tim was a chatterbox, hyperactive and go-go-go.' (p.164)

'[Sizwe] was that friend who believed in you and saw the potential in you that nobody else did …' (p.203)

Noah's childhood friends provide much of the humour in this text, from Noah's early school days through to his troubled adolescence and problems with the law. Of the friends Noah discusses in his memoir, three are remembered in particular detail, outlined below.

Teddy

Teddy is one of Noah's schoolfriends at Sandringham, and Noah describes him as 'funny … [and] charming as hell' (p.153). Teddy and Noah are incredibly close, always attached to one another and always getting into trouble. The story of their relationship, told in the chapter 'Colorblind', is used to highlight the systemic inequities and racism in post-apartheid South Africa. When Teddy and Noah are chased by security guards after stealing chocolates from a cinema, and Teddy is caught, the authorities are unable to identify Noah on the security footage because the grainy video tape makes him appear white next to his black friend.

Tim

Tim is described as a 'chatterbox' and 'hyperactive' (p.164). It is Tim who convinces Noah to invite Babiki to the matriculation dance, making a deal with him for a better cut on the profits from the bootleg CDs they are selling. Tim represents another of the young entrepreneurial characters who influenced Noah's life, and his story is also important to the ongoing circus of Noah's love life.

Sizwe

Sizwe is a popular boy who lives in the slums of Alexandra. Noah describes him as 'that friend who believed in you and saw the potential in you that nobody else did' (p.203). Like Tim, Sizwe is an intelligent and entrepreneurial character who introduces Noah to many of the realities of life in the hood. Together they launch an operation not only burning bootleg CDs, but also using the music and a dance crew to put on parties around Alex in order to make money. Again, Noah reflects on the importance of these friends in his young life, and in his journey out of poverty.

Key point

It is clear that Noah holds many of his memories of his friends very dear, and that he appreciates and respects the support they offer him. Although they often get him into trouble with the law, he learns a lot from his friends about how to survive in post-apartheid South Africa. Noah reinforces the idea that divisions of colour and race are ridiculous through his friends, who are white, black, coloured and Chinese.

THEMES, IDEAS & VALUES

Apartheid

Key quotes

'The genius of apartheid was convincing people who were the overwhelming majority to turn on each other.' (p.3)

'Apartheid was perfect racism.' (p.19)

'In South Africa, the atrocities of apartheid have never been taught that way. We weren't taught judgment or shame.' (p.183)

The discussion of apartheid – before, during and after – is key to *Born a Crime*, and is the reason for the title of the book. The text begins with an excerpt from the 1927 Immorality Act, which explains the 'crime' of being born to black and white parents. Noah reflects on this crime, commenting that, 'during apartheid, one of the worst crimes you could commit was having sexual relations with a person of another race' (p.21). Noah attributes this to the idea that race-mixing reveals institutional racism (like the laws of apartheid) as 'unsustainable and incoherent' (p.21), as people continue to have relationships based on simple human needs and desires, irrespective of race.

Apartheid is explored from a number of angles, primarily through the contextual pieces that precede each chapter, which provide historical discussions of the rationale for apartheid and the ways in which the laws came about. Noah calls apartheid 'perfect racism' (p.19) because it was a distillation of the most expedient racial laws from other countries, including the segregation of blacks and whites in the US, the treatment of First Nations Australians, the British slave trade and 'the racist policies of the Third Reich' (p.195). This is why Noah calls apartheid 'the most advanced system of racial oppression known to man' (p.19). Ultimately, apartheid 'convinced every group that it was because of the other race that they didn't get into the club' (p.120), turning each racial group against the others.

Apartheid was not only about division and segregation, however; it was also about displacing native Africans, stripping them of basic human rights and access to education and healthcare: 'The ultimate goal of apartheid was to make South Africa a white country, with every black person stripped of his or her citizenship and relocated to live in the homelands' (p.23). These non-white citizens were forced to live in slums like Soweto, which, with only two roads in and out, was designed to be bombed. Noah comments on how violence both within these slums and by a corrupt police force only exacerbated the issue. Having access to the worlds of white, black and coloured people, primarily through school, Noah can also see the other side of the injustice: the white people who are too comfortable with a system that privileges them and their children to act for what is right.

Noah also discusses the fall of apartheid as 'a gradual thing. It wasn't like the Berlin Wall where one day it just came down. Apartheid's walls cracked and crumbled over many years' (p.69). He tells the story from a unique perspective, pointing out that while the decline of apartheid after Nelson Mandela's release was called 'the Bloodless Revolution', 'black blood ran in the streets' (p.12). Following the end of apartheid, South African children were not taught about the atrocities of the time. Unlike German school students learning about the Holocaust, they were not taught 'judgment or shame'; they were simply told that 'apartheid was bad. Nelson Mandela was freed. Let's move on' (p.183). The reasons for this were to absolve the previous government and the non-white citizens who benefited from this system, as well as to ingrain the injustices that may no longer have been officially sanctioned by law but which continued to play out on the ground, particularly for black South Africans in the slums.

Race and colour

Key quotes

'In any society built on institutionalized racism, race-mixing doesn't merely challenge the system as unjust, it reveals the system as unsustainable and incoherent.' (p.21)

'Racism teaches us that we are different because of the color of our skin. But because racism is stupid, it's easily tricked.' (p.49)

'The history of colored people in South Africa is, in this respect, worse than the history of black people in South Africa. For all that black people have suffered, they know who they are. Colored people don't.' (p.116)

Throughout the text Noah speaks both of ethnic groups – for example, Xhosa and Zulu, African and Afrikaner – and of colour: black, white and coloured (mixed-race). At the start of the text Noah discusses the differences between the predominant black racial groups in Africa: the Xhosa, like his mother, were seen as a calmer and more intellectual group than the warrior-like Zulu, but stereotypes existed on both sides. These racial differences were used by the colonists to drive a wedge between black people and to make it easier to enforce segregation and other laws of apartheid.

On a number of occasions Noah reflects on both the problems and the advantages of being coloured. Because he is coloured, his family does 'what the American justice system does' and gives him 'more lenient treatment than the black kids' (p.52), which is how he escapes the beatings from his grandmother that his black cousins suffer. However, as a child Noah does not understand these racial differences, seeing different colours as 'all just chocolate' (p.54). It is not until he transfers to H. A. Jack Primary, a government school, that he feels like he is 'seeing [his] country for the first time' (p.57) – the divisions between black, white and other groups such as Indian and Chinese are now obvious to him. It is at this point that Noah decides that he identifies most with the black children, despite the fact that his mother had raised him 'like a white kid' (p.73), to believe that the world is his oyster.

As he grows older, Noah starts to appreciate more the challenges faced by black and coloured people in South Africa. He reflects that 'the history of colored people in South Africa is … worse than the history of black people in South Africa. For all that black people have suffered, they know who they are. Colored people don't' (p.116). Noah's lack of racial identity – stemming in part from his absent father and in part from his ostracism by other black children – leads to the confusing situation in which some people mistreat him for being black and others 'hated [him] because of [his] whiteness' (p.121). He also speaks to the absurdity of racism when he remembers the confusion of the school principal watching footage of him and a friend running from security guards on CCTV. Because the camera cannot pick up the contrast between Noah's light skin and his black friend, the authorities 'could not see that the white person they were looking for was sitting right in front of them' (p.159).

Poverty

Key quotes

'That is the curse of being black and poor, and it is a curse that follows you from generation to generation. My mother calls it "the black tax."' (p.66)

'I never felt poor because our lives were so rich with experience.' (p.72)

'The first thing I learned about having money was that it gives you choices. People don't want to be rich. They want to be able to choose.' (p.188)

The young Noah spends much of his life in poverty, even if he only realises this fact upon reflection as an adult. Remembering his childhood, Noah comments that 'whenever times were really tough we'd fall back on dog bones' (p.72), but even so he never 'felt poor' because his life growing up with his mother was 'so rich with experience' (p.72). There are moments throughout the text where it becomes apparent that growing up poor in South Africa was incredibly hard; however, Noah approaches the topic with his typical sense of humour. For example, unable to afford petrol, Noah remembers 'some of the most embarrassing shit, pushing the car to school like the fucking Flintstones' (pp.135–6).

Noah also reflects on the sociopolitical causes and effects of poverty, and the difference between being poor and having money. At school he feels an 'affinity' for the 'poor black kids' (pp.138–9), seeing the most similarities between their lives and his. He understands the subtle differences between families like Babiki's, who 'try to act like they're not' poor (p.168), and friends like Sizwe from the shanty township of Alexandra. Noah also provides a commentary on how a large number of black people in South Africa try to escape poverty, largely through 'hustling' and an entrepreneurial (or sometimes criminal) spirit. From a white boy, Andrew, he learns 'how important it is to empower the dispossessed and the disenfranchised in the wake of oppression' (p.190), and he also acknowledges that 'people don't want to be rich. They want to be able to choose' (p.188). Yet Noah concedes that it is almost impossible for black South Africans to 'make something of themselves' because they simply don't have the 'raw materials' (p.190). Exacerbating this issue are the remnants of the apartheid system, which precluded black people from gaining a proper education, owning businesses or learning languages other than their mother tongue. (Noah is a rare exception, with his impressive command of many languages one result of his mother's rebellious approach to the laws of apartheid.) The lasting effects of this era can be seen in the failure of the auto shop purchased by Abel, who is unaware that purchasing a business means taking on its debt. Thus, the cycle of poverty and limited opportunities continues for the vast majority of black people, who are unable to break free from a system designed to keep them down.

Some of Noah's most powerful recollections of poverty come from his time spent in 'the hood' with Sizwe, seeing firsthand the differences between even his own level of poverty and that of the people of Alex. In Alex, even something as seemingly ordinary as cheese is a status symbol, because it is the most expensive food item that can be added to an order. The 'cheese boys' label (p.207) is used both as praise and as an insult, with people drawing a line between the poor and the slightly less poor. In the hood, Noah notices that 'you're always working, working, working, and you feel like something's happening, but really nothing's happening at all', and that 'hustling is to work what surfing the Internet is to reading' (p.217) – i.e. you might consume hours' worth of information via Twitter and Facebook in a year, but that doesn't mean you've read any books. This analogy reinforces the idea that for all the hard work of life in Alexandra, people are merely surviving from day to day and never getting anywhere.

For Noah, comedy provides a way out of poverty; however, it is the skills and mindset he was imbued with as a child that allow him to leverage his sense of humour. He acknowledges that 'when I look back I realize [my mother] raised me like a white kid – not white culturally, but in the sense of believing that the world was my oyster' (p.73). Patricia's determination to have Noah see himself as 'equal' to white South Africans is one of the main factors in him ultimately escaping the poverty of her own life.

Crime, violence and the law

Key quotes

'In the hood, even if you're not a hardcore criminal, crime is in your life in some way or another.' (p.209)

'One day you're going to get arrested, and when you do, don't call me. I'll tell the police to lock you up just to teach you a lesson.' (Patricia, p.228)

'The case never went to trial. Abel pled guilty to attempted murder. He was given three years' probation. He didn't serve a single day in prison.' (p.284)

Like poverty – and often as a direct result of it – crime and violence are never far from Noah's stories. The beginning chapters in Part I of the book make some mention of the violence of apartheid and the so-called Bloodless Revolution, and Noah reflects on his 'animal instinct' in a world where 'violence was always lurking and waiting to erupt' (p.16); however, it is not until the latter parts of the book, as Noah heads into his teenage years, that the true violence of his childhood comes to the fore.

Entering Alexandra, Noah notes how the 'energy' of hundreds of thousands of people living on top of one another 'erupts periodically in epic acts of violence and crazy parties' (p.205). Like his discussion of poverty, the topic of crime and violence is often handled with a light touch and even humour. Noah thinks about the hustling in Alex, including his own selling of bootleg CDs, and acknowledges that 'none of it was legal' (p.212). And yet there is a feeling that much of the violence and crime in *Born a Crime* is not the fault of the perpetrators, but of the system. People commit crimes, ranging from petty to serious, simply in order to live and provide food and shelter for their families. When truly serious crimes are committed, the criminals are punished as much by the community as by the police, and sometimes more.

Noah has multiple encounters with the law throughout the book. His mother flatly informs him that 'one day you're going to get arrested' and that when he does she will leave him locked up to 'teach [him] a lesson' (p.228). Spending some time in jail after taking a car he did not know was stolen out for a joyride, Noah reflects that 'the law isn't rational at all. It's a lottery' and that imprisonment can be based on a series of seemingly unrelated questions such as 'What color is your skin? How much money do you have? Who's your lawyer? Who's the judge?' (p.238). Enforcing these irrational laws are the ever-present South African police. The system of policing in South Africa is seen partly as a result of apartheid, with a 'network of *impipis*, the anonymous snitches who'd inform on suspicious activity' (pp.29–30), and a suspicious environment where 'everyone thinks everyone else is the police' (p.25). The actual police are capable of as much callousness and corruption as anyone in the system, summed up by Patricia towards the end of the book: 'The world doesn't love you. If the police get you, the police don't love you. When I beat you, I'm trying to save you. When they beat you, they're trying to kill you' (p.243).

Despite being surrounded by violence and suffering mistreatment at the hands of the police, Noah 'was never violent at all' (p.262). His distaste for violence becomes even more apparent as he closes the book with his memories of possibly the most violent person in his life: Abel. Noah 'saw the futility of violence, the cycle that just repeats itself, the damage that's inflicted on people that they in turn inflict on others' (p.262). He sees how violence in retaliation for Abel's abusive relationship with his mother will not solve anything. Even after the violent climax of the book, when Abel shoots Patricia in the leg and head, Noah does not resort to violence himself. Ultimately, Noah escapes the violence of his own childhood in much the same way he frees himself from poverty: through his humour and intellect.

Language and education

Key quotes

'Everyone knows that Jesus, who's white, speaks English. The Bible is in English. Yes, the Bible was not *written* in English, but the Bible came to South Africa in English so to us it's in English. Which made my prayers the best prayers because English prayers get answered first.' (p.40)

'"It does not serve the Bantu to learn history and science because he is primitive," the government said.' (p.61)

'Nelson Mandela once said, "If you talk to a man in a language he understands, that goes to his head. If you talk to him in his language, that goes to his heart."' (p.236)

Language and education are both seen as means of building understanding and bridging the manmade divide between races, repairing some of the damage of apartheid. However, they are also both used as tools of apartheid, with language deployed as one of the dividing forces and education denied to black children in order to keep them oppressed.

Education – or the denial of it – was a tool used by the oppressors in South Africa to disenfranchise black people. During apartheid, the authorities created Bantu schools, which were extremely limited in curriculum because the government declared that 'it does not serve the Bantu to learn history and science because [they are] primitive' (p.61). Noah reflects on the difference between apartheid and other forms of racism when he states, 'British racism said, "If the monkey can walk like a man and talk like a man, then perhaps he is a man." Afrikaner racism said, "Why give a book to a monkey?"' (p.62). The entire system of apartheid was designed to strip power away from the black majority so that, like the huge and terrifying but gentle man Noah later meets in prison, they lack 'the tools necessary to cope with' the world (p.237).

Noah's own education, with his experiences at various primary schools and high schools, is an important part of the text. However, Noah's anecdotes often revolve around aspects of school life that have nothing to do with education, such as his constant pranks and misbehaviour, or the ruthless punishments by the teachers. Speaking about Catholic school, Noah notes that discipline was 'no joke' (p.85) and states, 'Catholic school is similar to apartheid in that it's ruthlessly authoritarian, and its authority rests on a bunch of rules that don't make any sense' (p.88). In fact, for Noah, he learned much more from his mother and from his life hustling on the streets of Alexandra than he did in school. His mother 'taught [him] how to think' (p.68), and instilled in him a love of books and learning that existed independently of the classroom.

From a young age, Noah was also gifted with languages. His mother taught him English as his first language, a skill that became useful even when praying, because as Noah says humorously, 'Everyone knows that Jesus, who's white, speaks English' (p.40). Reflecting on the power of language, Noah writes that language brings 'an identity and a culture' and that 'a shared language says "We're the same." A language barrier says "We're different"' (p.49). He uses his grasp of language to confuse bullies, befriend people and navigate the complex 'Tower of Babel' (p.161) of post-apartheid South Africa, where many different language speakers mix together. For example, when a group of Zulu guys tries to mug him, Noah overhears them speaking to each other in their native tongue. Believing that he is white and will not understand them, they are shocked when Noah turns around and says in Zulu, 'Yo, guys, why don't we just mug someone together?' (p.55). After hearing Noah speak their language, they accept him as one of their own, explaining that they 'were trying to steal from white people' (p.56). This incident reveals to Noah that 'language, even more than color, defines who you are to people' (p.56).

Relationships

Key quotes

'[Dinky] was trying to live up to this image of what he thought a husband should be, dominant, controlling. I remember being told as a child, "If you don't hit your woman, you don't love her."' (p.37)

'As a nation, we recognized the power of women, but in the home they were expected to submit and obey.' (p.39)

'What I learned was that cool guys get girls, and funny guys get to hang out with the cool guys with their girls.' (p.146)

Although *Born a Crime* focuses on serious, large-scale issues relating to apartheid, race and colour, poverty, and crime and violence, it also explores the human element underpinning these themes: relationships between individuals and groups.

Women and men

Throughout *Born a Crime* Noah explores the relationships between women and men in South African society, both in terms of patriarchal African customs and in post-apartheid South Africa. As with many ideas in the text, Noah's thoughts on the roles of women and men in society are heavily influenced by his mother, who tells him that 'being a man is not what you have, it's who you are. Being more of a man doesn't mean your woman has to be less than you' (p.127). This message is reflected in Noah's descriptions of family members like his uncle Dinky, who was 'trying to live up to this image of what he thought a husband should be, dominant, controlling' (p.37), and the abusive and violent Abel. There is also violence perpetrated by women against men, with boiling water used as a weapon to teach a man 'a lesson' and boiling oil used 'to end it' (p.37). With these experiences growing up, it is unsurprising that Noah finds his own relationships challenging and confusing.

Romance

Noah's romantic experiences are recounted with humour, particularly in Part II of the book, in which he reflects on his adolescence. His first failed romantic relationship stems from being matched with a coloured girl because it is his *'responsibility'* (p.130) to ask her out. As the *'only two'* (p.130) coloured children, they are paired up by their friends, with little say themselves. Ultimately, the girl dumps Noah before they even have a chance to go on a date, having been asked out by one of the popular white boys.

As he reaches the senior years, Noah reflects that 'in high school, the attention of girls was not an affliction [he] suffered from' (p.145). Admitting defeat, he resigns himself to playing the role of the funny guy, knowing that 'cool guys get girls, and funny guys get to hang out with the cool guys with their girls' (p.146). This is a message that is repeated several times throughout the book and speaks to how important a sense of humour is in Noah's life. After failing to ask out Zaheera, a friend he had a crush on but who moved to the US before he could muster up the courage to reveal his feelings, Noah's next romantic encounter is with Babiki, who Noah eventually discovers does not speak any English. That story concludes with the comment that he had 'spent four years of high school carefully avoiding any kind of romantic humiliation whatsoever, and now, on the night of the matric dance, the night of all nights, [his] humiliation had turned into a circus bigger than the event itself' (p.176).

Friendship

Born a Crime is filled with stories of the friendships Noah had growing up, many of which involved crimes and misdemeanours. Friends such as Tim, Sizwe and Teddy appear throughout the book, usually in anecdotes about Noah's scrapes with the law. Noah reflects on the challenges of making friends as a coloured boy in South Africa, not really fitting in with either the black or white children. He remarks that 'the key to making black friends in the suburbs [is] the children of domestics' (p.152), adding an element of his discussions of class and poverty to the exploration of relationships.

DIFFERENT INTERPRETATIONS

Different interpretations arise from different responses to a text. Over time, a text will evoke a wide range of responses from its readers, who may come from various social or cultural groups and live in very different places and historical periods. Responses by critics and reviewers can be published in newspapers, journals and books, both online and in print. They can also be expressed in discussions among readers in the media, classrooms, book groups and so on.

While there is no single correct reading or interpretation of a text, it is important to understand that an interpretation is more than a personal opinion – it is the justification of a point of view on the text. To present an interpretation of a text based on your point of view, you must use a logical argument and support it with relevant evidence from the text.

Critical viewpoints

Reviews of Trevor Noah's memoir have been largely favourable, often focusing on his wit and humour, and the rawness of his storytelling. Writing for *The New York Times*, Kakutani refers to the text as 'alarming, sad and funny' (Kakutani 2016), commenting on the 'sharp-edged snapshots' Noah provides of his life growing up in South Africa. Kakutani also highlights the more positive qualities of Noah's childhood, as well as the way the text functions as a 'love letter to the author's remarkable mother', Patricia. In a separate interview with *New York Times* writer Maria Russo, Noah speaks about the young readers' adaptation of *Born a Crime*, in which some of the more violent content and coarse language was removed. He refers to the importance of not diluting the message of the story, stating that many stories for children have 'complicated ideas children can grasp if the storyteller relates to [them] in an authentic way' (Russo 2019).

Similarly positive, *The Guardian* refers to Noah's text as 'an engaging, fast-paced and vivid read', written 'with characteristic insight and humour' (Thamm 2016). Commenting on the deeply personal nature of the stories, the review labels the text as 'essential reading not only because it is a personal story of survival, leavened with insight and wit, but because it does more to expose apartheid – its legacy, its pettiness, its small-minded stupidity and its damage – than any other recent history book or academic text'.

Other reviews of the book focus even more on the uplifting aspects of the text, with *Live Wire* referring to it as an 'accidental ode to his remarkable mother' and highlighting the 'restorative qualities of love and joy' (Panesar 2019) in Noah's stories. Black history and literature website *Noire Histoir* also discusses the positive impact of Noah's discussions of apartheid, outlining a 'shared history' of black people's struggles (McEachron 2019).

Despite the overwhelmingly positive reviews, the book has not been without controversy – mostly due to the sometimes controversial nature of Noah himself. A school in Needham, in the US, banned the book following some of Noah's commentary on the 2021 Palestine–Israel conflict (Ballantyne 2021; McLean 2021). However, it is worth noting that the removal of Noah's book from shelves was labelled as 'whitewashing': attempting to remove important historical facts to present white history in a more favourable light.

Ultimately, Noah's book has been both well received and lauded as an important text in highlighting the atrocities of the apartheid and post-apartheid eras in South Africa.

Two possible interpretations

The following interpretations demonstrate how contrasting viewpoints about a text can be valid, as long as they are supported by evidence from that text.

Interpretation 1: *Born a Crime* shows that Trevor Noah's childhood was incredibly harsh and filled with violence and struggle.

It is certainly possible to read Trevor Noah's memoir and focus on all the dangerous, violent and sometimes terrifying events of his childhood. From the very start of the text there is a threatening undertone, with even the title demonstrating that Noah's birth was criminal. Beginning with an extract from the 1927 Immorality Act and moving quickly onto the laws preventing racial mixing, Noah shows how his childhood was never going to be easy.

Even though the 'atrocities of apartheid' (p.183) had never been taught to children in South Africa, Noah lived through their effects. His mother's poverty, the struggles he faced as a coloured boy growing up in South Africa, and the lengths his mother had to go to in order to provide him with a good upbringing were all a result of the lasting effects of apartheid.

Because of his colour and low socioeconomic status, Noah spent much of his time mixing with other children and young adults who were either criminals themselves or turned a blind eye to criminal activities. Noah was himself responsible for many crimes, including selling bootlegged CDs and stolen goods. The fact that he never viewed these actions as criminal – at least until he discovered a digital camera filled with a family's holiday photos – demonstrates that crime was seen as a normal part of life. For someone growing up in South Africa, Noah reflects, 'crime is in your life in some way or another' (p.209).

Noah also dwells on the periodic 'epic acts of violence' that occurred in places like Alex as a result of the 'energy' (p.205) of thousands of people living in such close, impoverished quarters. In addition to crime, he experienced violence as a part of his daily life throughout his childhood. After apartheid ended, 'black blood ran in the streets' (p.12) and Noah recalls seeing the rising daily death toll: 'A dozen people killed. Fifty people killed. A hundred people killed' (p.12). He reflects on his 'animal instincts' as a child, 'learned in a world where violence was always lurking' (p.16). Ultimately, when his stepfather Abel beats his mother, first with his fists, then with a bicycle, leading up to him shooting her in the leg and back of the head, the violence in Noah's life escalates to an almost unbelievable point. These incidents show that, as a result of systemic issues that were far beyond his control, Noah's childhood was filled with violence, desperation and poverty.

Interpretation 2: *Born a Crime* shows that Trevor Noah's childhood, though not without adversity, was filled with moments of humour and joy.

Despite the obvious horrors of his childhood – including extreme poverty, crime and violence – *Born a Crime* is filled with moments of comedy, joy and love. Throughout the memoir Noah makes light of situations that seem horrific. Approaching his turbulent childhood with a sense of humour, Noah demonstrates that growing up in South Africa was challenging, but he did not let those challenges define his life.

Although Noah grew up surrounded by crime, he remembers his childhood misdemeanours more for the friendships he formed and the fun he had. Reflecting on friends like Sizwe, with whom he ran a bootleg CD and dance party empire, Noah clearly thinks fondly of many of his childhood experiences. Getting into trouble with Teddy, including Teddy's arrest after getting caught by security guards, is recounted as a hilarious anecdote rather than a serious or shameful memory. As Noah reflects, he 'never once thought of [hustling] as a crime' and 'honestly didn't think it was bad' (p.221) to sell stolen goods. The focus is much more on the friendships formed through his adverse upbringing than on the negative impacts of crime in his life.

His friends also introduce him to – often comically bad – relationships with girls such as Babiki, Maylene and Zaheera. Throughout the text he reflects on these failed relationships with humour, even including three similarly titled chapters on 'affairs of the heart' in Part II of the book, like episodes in a series. His relationship with his mother also brings a great deal of lightness and joy to the text, and despite their 'very Tom and Jerry relationship' (p.11), there is clearly a great deal of love. In spite of her own hardships, and the laws preventing race-mixing, Patricia 'chose to have' Noah (p.64) and raised him as best she could. She ensured that he had access to an education, knew how to speak English and had his 'spirit' (p.71) filled with both religious and life experiences.

In spite of the violence Noah witnessed growing up, he was 'never violent at all' and saw only the 'futility' of the 'cycle that just repeats itself' (p.262). Distancing himself from the violence inflicted on his mother by Abel, Noah acknowledges that growing up amid violence did not turn him into an aggressive person, nor did it ultimately strip away his sense of humour.

Ultimately, the love of his friends and family, his entrepreneurial spirit and his sense of humour meant that, despite the circumstances, Noah's childhood was still filled with moments of joy.

QUESTIONS & ANSWERS

This section focuses on your own analytical writing on the text, and gives you strategies for producing high-quality responses in your coursework and exam essays.

Essay writing – an overview

An essay on a literary work is a formal and serious piece of writing that presents your point of view on the text, usually in response to a given topic. Your 'point of view' in an essay is your interpretation of the meaning of the text's language, structure, characters, situations and events, supported by detailed analysis of textual evidence.

Analyse – don't summarise

In your essays it is important to avoid simply summarising what happens in a text.

- A **summary** is a description or paraphrase (retelling in different words) of the characters and events. For example: 'Macbeth has a horrifying vision of a dagger dripping with blood before he goes to murder King Duncan.'
- An **analysis** is an explanation of the real meaning or significance that lies 'beneath' the text's words (and images, for a film). For example: 'Macbeth's vision of a bloody dagger shows how deeply uneasy he is about the violent act he is contemplating, and conveys his sense that supernatural forces are impelling him to act.'

A limited amount of summary is sometimes necessary to let your reader know which part of the text you wish to discuss. However, always keep this to a minimum and follow it immediately with your analysis of what this part of the text is really telling us.

Plan your essay

Carefully plan your essay so that you have a clear idea of what you are going to say. The plan ensures that your ideas flow logically, that your argument remains consistent and that you stay on the topic. An essay plan should be a list of **brief dot points** covering no more than half a page.

- Include your central argument or main contention – a concise statement of your overall response to the topic.
- Write three or four dot points for each paragraph, indicating the main idea and evidence/examples from the text. In your essay you will need to *expand* on these points and *analyse* the evidence.

Structure your essay

An essay is a complete, self-contained piece of writing. It has a clear beginning (the introduction), middle (several body paragraphs) and end (the last paragraph or conclusion). It must also have a central argument that runs throughout, linking each paragraph to form a coherent whole. See examples of introductions and conclusions in the 'Analysing a sample topic' and 'Sample answer' sections.

The introduction establishes your overall response to the topic. It includes your main contention and outlines the main evidence you will refer to in the course of the essay. Write your introduction *after* you have done a plan and *before* you write the rest of the essay.

The body paragraphs argue your case – they present evidence from the text and explain how this evidence supports your argument. Each body paragraph needs:

- a strong **topic sentence** (usually the first sentence) that states the main point being made in the paragraph
- **evidence** from the text, including some brief quotations
- **analysis** of the textual evidence, with **explanation** of its significance and how it supports your argument
- **links back to the topic** in one or more statements, usually towards the end of the paragraph.

Connect the body paragraphs so that your discussion flows smoothly. Use some linking words and phrases such as 'similarly' and 'on the other hand', though don't start every paragraph like this. Another strategy is to use a significant word from the last sentence of one paragraph in the first sentence of the next.

Use key terms from the topic – or synonyms for them – throughout, so the relevance of your discussion to the topic is always clear.

The conclusion ties everything together and finishes the essay. It includes strong statements that emphasise your central argument and provide a clear response to the topic.

Avoid simply restating the points made earlier in the essay – this will end on a very flat note and imply that you have run out of ideas and vocabulary. The conclusion should be a logical extension of what you have written, not just a repetition or summary of it. Writing an effective conclusion can be a challenge. Try using these tips:

- Start by linking back to the final sentence of the second-last paragraph, rather than leaping to your main contention straight away – this helps your writing to flow.
- Use synonyms and expressions with equivalent meanings to vary your vocabulary. This allows you to reinforce your line of argument without being repetitive.
- When planning your essay, think of one or two broad statements or observations about the text's wider meaning. These should be related to the topic and your overall argument. Keep them for the conclusion, since they will give you something 'new' to say but still follow logically from your discussion. The introduction will be focused on the topic, but the conclusion can present a wider view of the text.

Essay topics

1 'In *Born a Crime*, Trevor Noah suggests that the law is often open to interpretation.' Do you agree?

2 "I learned that even though I didn't belong to one group, I could be a part of any group that was laughing."
Discuss the importance of humour in this text.

3 'Trevor Noah's book is as much a tragedy as it is a comedy.'
To what extent do you agree?

4 How does Trevor Noah explore the challenges of growing up coloured in post-apartheid South Africa?

5 "I saw the futility of violence, the cycle that just repeats itself ..."
Discuss the impact of violence on Trevor Noah's childhood.

6 "She never let me see us as victims. We were victims, me and my mom, Andrew and Isaac. Victims of apartheid. Victims of abuse. But I was never allowed to think that way, and I didn't see her life that way."
To what extent were Trevor Noah and his family victims?

7 How do the political and social impacts of apartheid echo throughout this text?

8 'Colour is just as important as ethnicity in *Born a Crime*.'
Do you agree?

9 'Trevor Noah explores the complexities of relationships between men and women in South Africa.' Discuss.

10 "I never felt poor because our lives were so rich with experience."
Did Trevor Noah suffer because of the poverty of his youth?

Vocabulary for writing on *Born a Crime*

Apartheid: A system of laws imposed in South Africa from 1948 until the 1990s that forced the segregation of whites and non-whites and denied non-white citizens basic human rights.

Colour: The grouping of people based on skin colour.

Memoir: A form of nonfiction text in which the author writes factually about their own life and memories.

Race: The grouping of people based on a shared culture, history and language (also known as **ethnicity**).

Segregation: The separation of different peoples – often by force – based on race, religion, ethnicity and/or colour.

Analysing a sample topic

'In *Born a Crime*, Trevor Noah suggests that the law is often open to interpretation.' Do you agree?

When analysing an essay topic, it is important to understand precisely *what* the topic is asking you to do. This means identifying key words and terms, as well as task words such as 'discuss' and 'explore'. In the case of this topic, the type of question is 'Do you agree?'. This means that you will need to explore the topic from multiple angles but ultimately *resolve the tension* in the topic and answer the question. This topic also contains two key phrases or ideas to focus on, outlined below.

- **The law:** You will need to demonstrate an understanding of what 'the law' means in this text. That might include the laws of apartheid, which prevented racial mixing and led to Noah being 'born a crime'. It might also include laws governing the kinds of crime committed by Noah in his youth, such as selling bootleg CDs and stolen goods. Noah also discusses the failure of the law in South Africa to protect people – particularly women in abusive relationships, like his mother – and the bias, even in the post-apartheid era, against black, coloured and other non-white people.
- **Open to interpretation:** The phrase 'open to interpretation' means that an individual may have a different opinion to the law as written, or as upheld by authority figures and institutions such as the police. Individual interpretations of the law – most notably Noah's

own – appear throughout the book. Noah and his friends clearly do not see their actions as immoral, even if they acknowledge they are illegal. Similarly, the police allow certain illegal actions – such as Abel's abusive violence – because of patriarchal norms in the society.

To explore this topic from multiple angles, consider who is making and enforcing the laws, and who is breaking them. You might also discuss who benefits from or is disadvantaged by the laws, which may have societal, economic or racial implications. For example, do certain laws favour or disadvantage the poor? Non-whites? Men over women? Viewing the topic through these different lenses will allow for a robust and sophisticated response.

As discussed above, a 'Do you agree?' question ultimately necessitates an answer: you will need to conclude with a statement of either yes or no, supported by appropriate evidence from the text.

Sample introduction

> Trevor Noah's *Born a Crime* exposes the flaws in the South African legal system, and the ways in which its laws were open to interpretation. Covering periods both during and after apartheid, Noah's funny but often brutal account explores how laws disadvantaged certain groups of people, especially those who were black, coloured and/or poor. Through the humorous stories of his childhood and adolescent misdemeanours, Noah demonstrates both his and others' interpretations of crime and the law, and how the laws were applied to him. Furthermore, the way in which authority figures and institutions interpreted the law frequently failed people like him, his mother and others in South African society.

Body paragraph outline

Paragraph 1: Noah demonstrates that he has his own interpretations of the law.

- Throughout the text Noah is frequently involved in criminal activities; his crimes include producing bootleg CDs, buying and selling stolen goods and holding illegal street parties. There is also the more serious crime of burning down a house.
- Throughout the text, Noah maintains that he doesn't see his activities – even the accidental burning down of the house – as criminal. He justifies his reasons in various ways, including that he acted out of necessity because of his poverty.

Paragraph 2: Others in the text view the law in a similar way to Noah.

- Many of Noah's friends are involved in the criminal activities he discusses from his youth and seem to share his view that these actions are not wrong or worthy of retribution, but simply part of their lives.
- Noah reflects that the places in which he grew up were filled with 'criminals' of various levels, from petty thieves to murderers. He discusses how, in places like Alexandra, crime was a relatively normal way of life, with mothers buying obviously stolen goods because of their lower prices, and everybody hustling just to survive.

Paragraph 3: The law is interpreted by those supposed to uphold it, often to the detriment of people like Noah and his family.

- The law frequently fails to protect those around Noah. In particular, the acceptance of Abel's abuse by the local police is one of the factors that contribute to his mother's shooting.
- The law fails to protect certain groups of people, discriminating on the grounds of race and colour.
- Post-apartheid South African laws failed to redress the great wrongs done to non-whites during the period of segregation, and in some cases compounded the problems.

Sample conclusion

Throughout *Born a Crime* Trevor Noah reflects on the various interpretations and failures of the law. During apartheid, many laws were put in place to segregate people and strip away their rights. Following the end of apartheid, however, the effects of racism and the barriers facing people from poor backgrounds remained. Noah argues that his actions as a youth were not criminal because they were driven by economic necessity and his entrepreneurial spirit. Similarly, he argues that in places like the slums of Alexandra, crime was simply a way of life, and a by-product of societal pressures. Ultimately, Noah suggests that the laws in South Africa during his childhood were open to interpretation and were not sufficient to protect the most vulnerable members of society.

SAMPLE ANSWER

How do the political and social impacts of apartheid echo throughout this text?

In *Born a Crime* the after-effects of apartheid are felt on both an individual and a societal level. The laws and regulations put in place in 1948, and lasting for almost fifty years, had a dramatic impact on all South Africans, but particularly black and coloured people. Noah, being born of a black mother and white father, was proof of the 'crime' of race-mixing. Throughout his memoir he demonstrates the lasting impact of apartheid on South African society, including the lack of access to education, generational poverty and the effects of racism. Even though apartheid ended when Noah was still a child, it is clear that it has also impacted his whole life.

Designed as 'the most advanced system of racial oppression known to man' and drawing on multiple existing forms of segregation from other nations, apartheid made it incredibly difficult for black people in South Africa to access an education. Even after apartheid ended, there were generations of black people who suffered as a result of the policies and beliefs that had been in place for decades. Labelling the Bantu or black peoples as 'primitive', the authorities who put apartheid in place denied them access to subjects such as 'history and science' in favour of sing-song lessons of little value. Noah comments that, as opposed to the way 'British racism' allowed for a black person to gain an education and therefore elevate their position, 'Afrikaner racism said, "Why give a book to a monkey?"' It is for this reason that Noah's mother works so hard to ensure her son has access to a quality education and encourages his reading and learning at home. Towards the end of the memoir, during his time in a jail cell, Noah meets a man who 'has no education' and 'no skills'; because he grew up in apartheid, the man has 'none of the tools necessary to cope' with the world. This example clearly shows that one of the lasting legacies of apartheid in South Africa was the inequalities caused by a lack of education.

Another of the inequalities created by apartheid that continues long beyond Noah's childhood is the wealth divide between black and white people. Noah writes frequently about his poverty growing up, reflecting on how his family would 'fall back on dog bones' as food and how wealth in the 'hood' of Alexandra was measured by the ability to afford extra cheese on a meal. Noah reflects on the poverty of black and coloured people in South Africa as a legacy of apartheid. He learns, from a white friend who gives him a CD burner, 'how important it is to empower the dispossessed and the disenfranchised in the wake of oppression'. He also understands that, for most black people in South Africa, empowerment never happens, which is why hustling and crime is a way of life in places such as Alex. Noah's mother calls this 'the black tax': the 'curse of being black and poor', as it echoes through families from 'generation to generation'.

The text suggests that the greatest impact of apartheid in South Africa was the systemic and pervasive racism that negatively affected all non-white citizens. Calling apartheid 'perfect racism', Noah remembers that even after apartheid ended, 'black blood ran in the streets'. This was because one of the fundamental aims of apartheid was to pit different ethnic communities – such as the Xhosa and the Zulu – against one another. Apartheid not only enshrined racism into the culture of South Africa, it also amplified the tensions between black people. Apartheid also drew further divisions between black people and coloured people, with Noah reflecting on ridiculous laws that could allow a person to be reclassified as white if they appeared white enough. Even though in his own childhood Noah viewed people of different colours 'like chocolate', he remembers that 'other people hated [him] because of his whiteness', and there are many occasions on which he is forced to 'pick a side'. Noah also reflects that coloured people in South Africa are a 'hybrid' people who don't 'know who they are', and so lack a place in society. This goes to show that one of the most lasting impacts of apartheid in South Africa is the racial divisions caused, not just between black people and white people, but between all races and ethnic groups.

In his memoir, Noah demonstrates that the impact of apartheid echoed long after its official end in 1994. Despite claims of a 'Bloodless Revolution', apartheid had antagonised existing tribal divisions and caused long-lasting racial issues between all the citizens of South Africa. Because of a lack of access to education, and deliberate moves by the authorities to deny black people basic human rights, generations of black and non-white families in South Africa grew up in poverty like Noah and his mother. Ultimately, the effects of the segregation will continue to echo long into the future, and texts like *Born a Crime* give just a small glimpse into the reality of people who grew up during and after apartheid.

REFERENCES

Text

Noah, T 2016, *Born a Crime: Stories from a South African Childhood,* John Murray (Publishers), London.

References

Alexander, M 2021, 'The 11 languages of South Africa', South Africa Gateway, https://southafrica-info.com/arts-culture/11-languages-south-africa/

Ballantyne, T 2021, 'Needham schools remove Trevor Noah's book from summer reading assignment', *Wicked Local,* 7 July, https://www.wickedlocal.com/story/needham-times/2021/07/07/needham-schools-cancel-trevor-noahs-book-required-summe-reading/7890183002

Encyclopedia Britannica 2022, 'Nelson Mandela', https://www.britannica.com/biography/Nelson-Mandela

Encyclopedia Britannica 2022, 'Trevor Noah', https://www.britannica.com/biography/Trevor-Noah

Kakutani, M 2016, '"Born a crime," Trevor Noah's raw account of life under apartheid', *The New York Times*, 28 November.

Malik, K 2021, 'Gross inequality stoked the violence in South Africa. It's a warning to us all', *The Guardian*, 18 July, https://www.theguardian.com/commentisfree/2021/jul/18/gross-inequality-stoked-violence-south-africa-warning-to-us-all

McEachron, N 2019, 'Born a Crime [Book review]', Noire History, https://noirehistoir.com/blog/born-a-crime-book-review

McLean, J 2021, 'Trevor Noah book about apartheid among 3 removed from Putnam reading list after outcry', *News4JAX,* 28 June, https://www.news4jax.com/news/local/2021/06/28/trevor-noah-book-about-apartheid-among-3-removed-from-putnam-reading-list-after-outcry

Panesar, A 2019, 'Book review | Trevor Noah's "Born a Crime" is an accidental ode to his remarkable mother', *Live Wire*, 12 May, https://livewire.thewire.in/out-and-about/books/book-review-trevor-noahs-born-a-crime-is-an-accidental-ode-to-his-remarkable-mother

Russo, M 2019, 'Trevor Noah thinks kids can handle the truth', *The New York Times*, 26 April.

Thamm, M 2016, 'Born a Crime: Trevor Noah charts his rise from South Africa's townships', *The Guardian*, 26 November, https://www.theguardian.com/world/2016/nov/25/born-a-crime-trevor-noah-south-africa-townships-daily-show